AN OLD-FASHIONED CHRISTMAS
COLORING BOOK

TED MENTEN

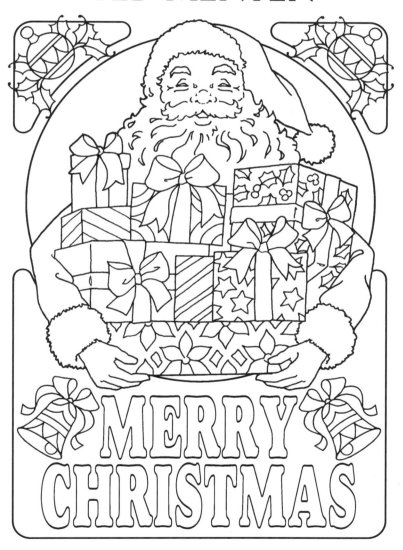

DOVER PUBLICATIONS, INC.
MINEOLA, NEW YORK

The most wonderful time of the year is on display in this charming collection. These 31 traditional designs will transport you to a day gone by, when carolers warmed hearts and ladies and gentlemen skated arm in arm on a nearby frozen pond. You'll be filled with joy as you flip through pages filled with candy canes, festive wreaths, gifts adorned with bows, and Santa himself! Designed for experienced colorists, the illustrations in this book will put you in the holiday spirit as you experiment with any color and media you wish. Each of the plates has been perforated for easy removal and display.

Bibliographical Note
An Old-Fashioned Christmas Coloring Book is a new work,
first published by Dover Publications, Inc., in 2016.

International Standard Book Number
ISBN-13: 978-0-486-81236-6
ISBN-10: 0-486-81236-7

Manufactured in the United States by LSC Communications
81236702   2016
www.doverpublications.com

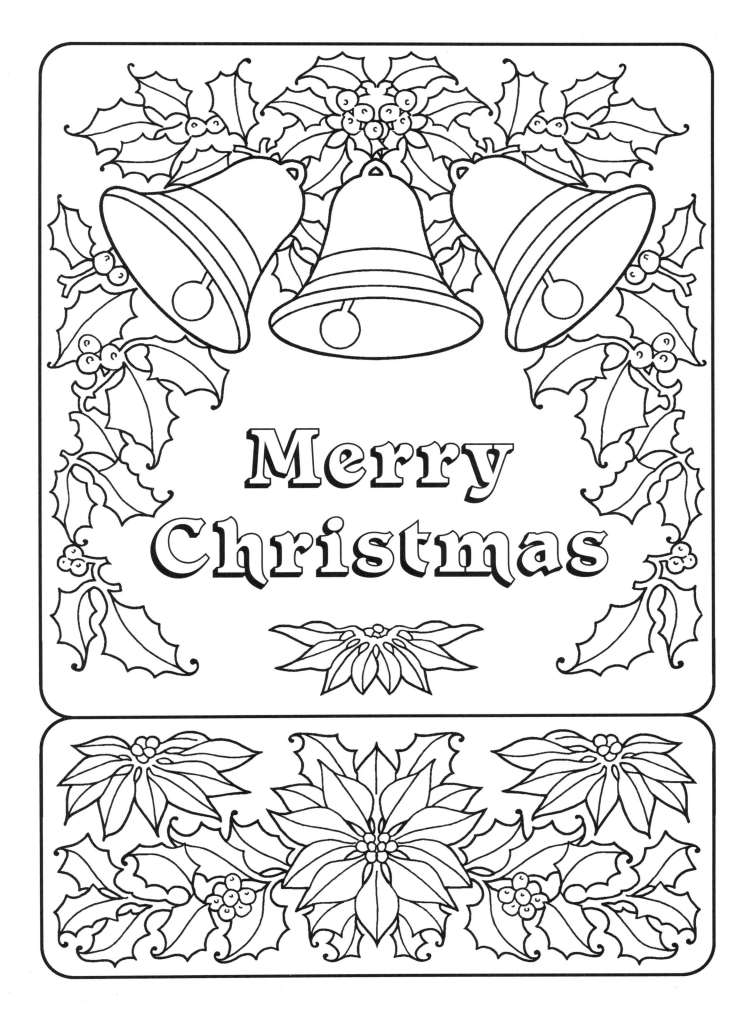

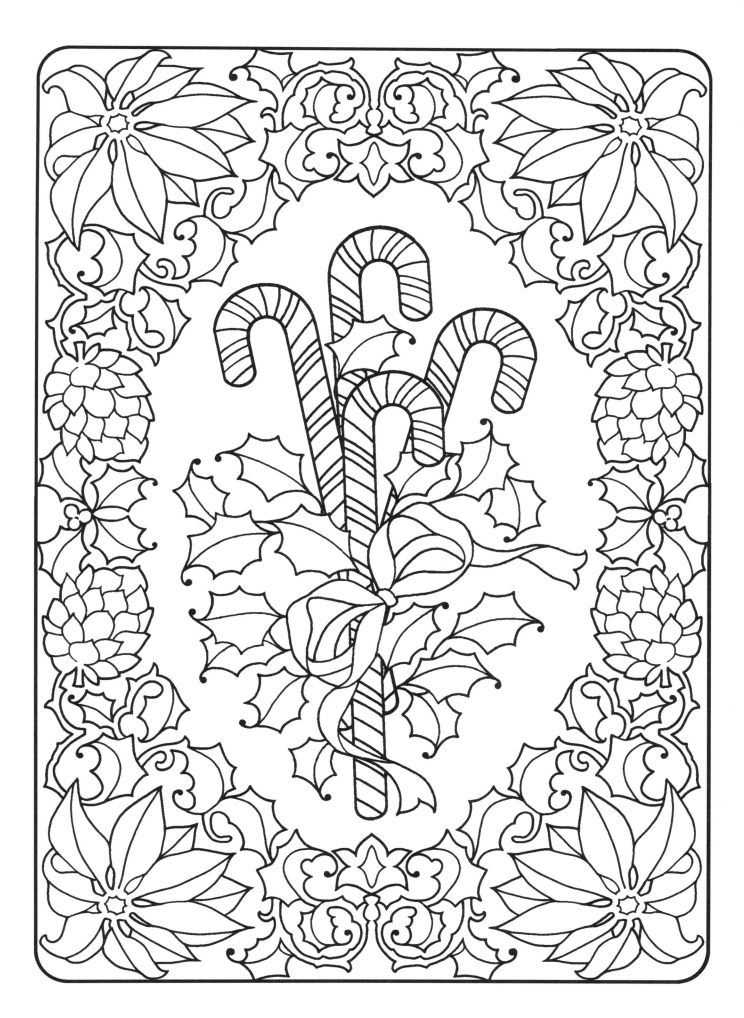

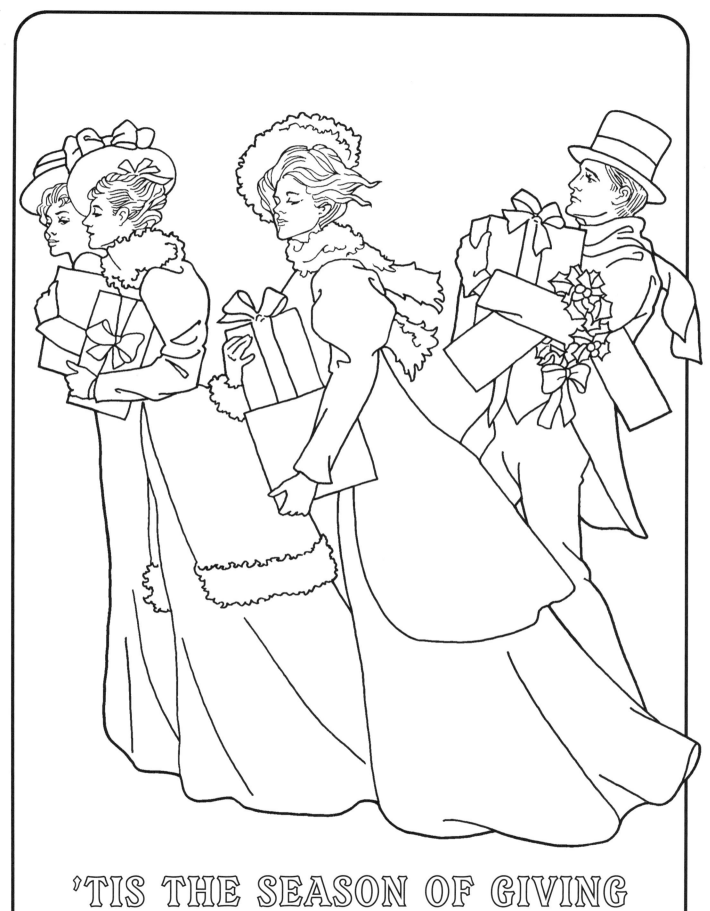

'TIS THE SEASON OF GIVING

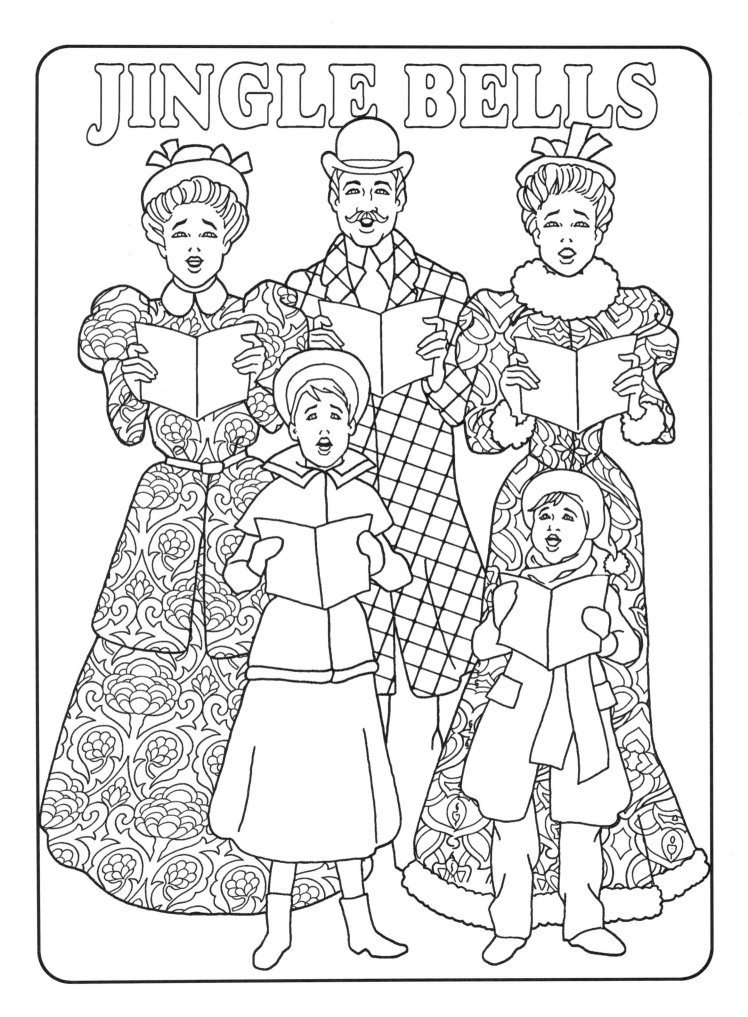

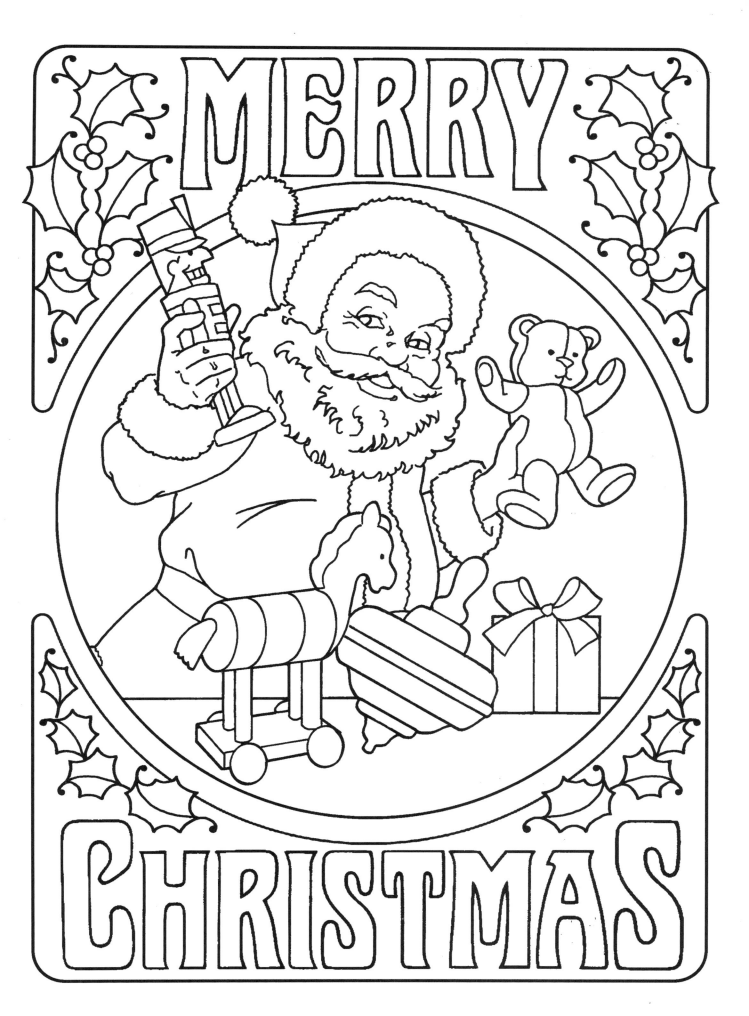

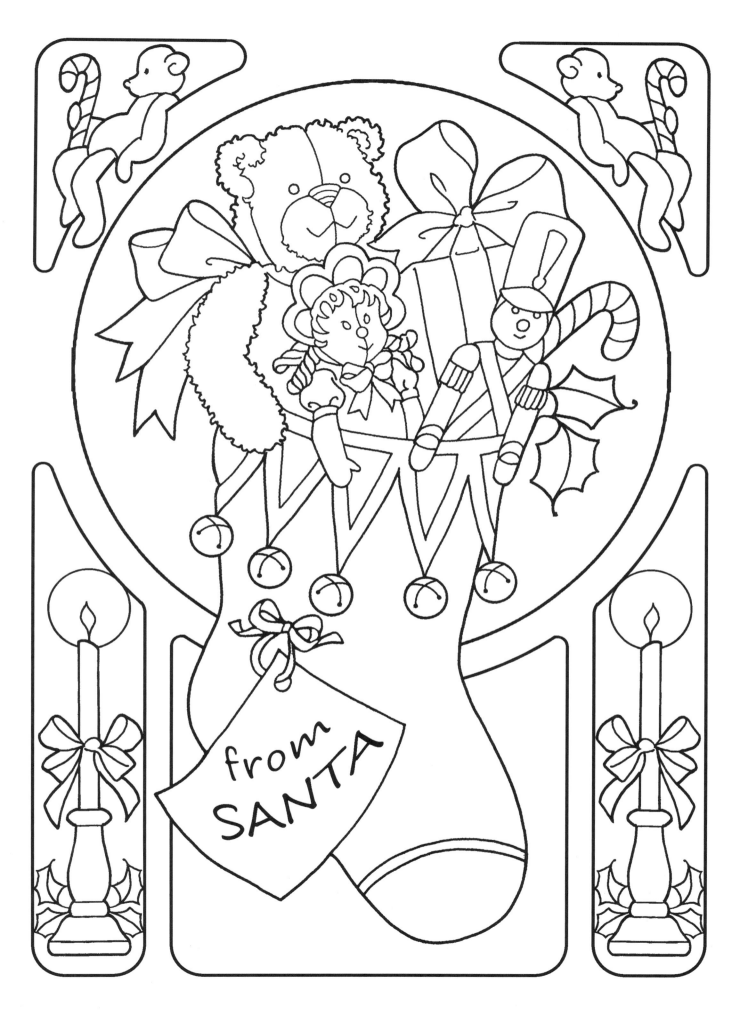

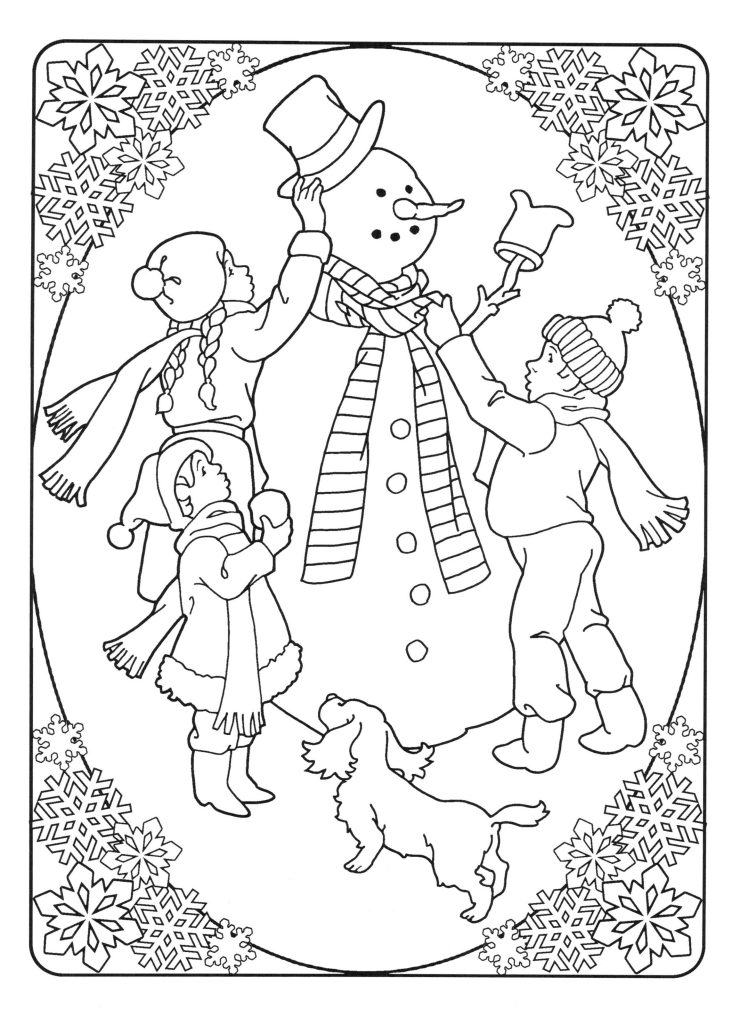

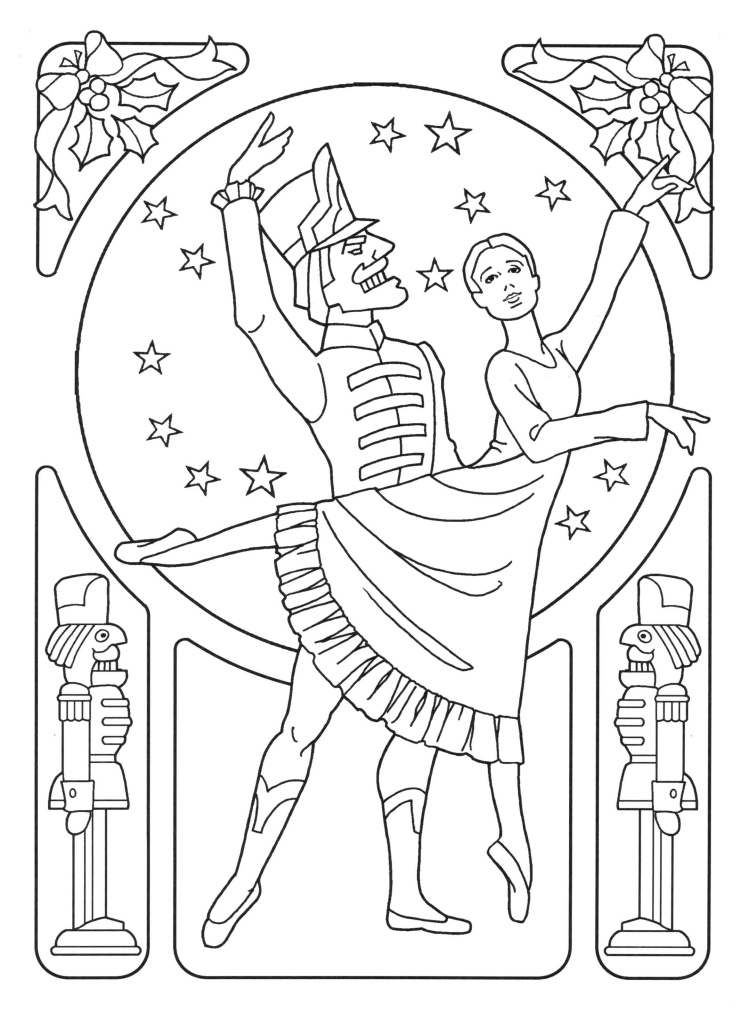

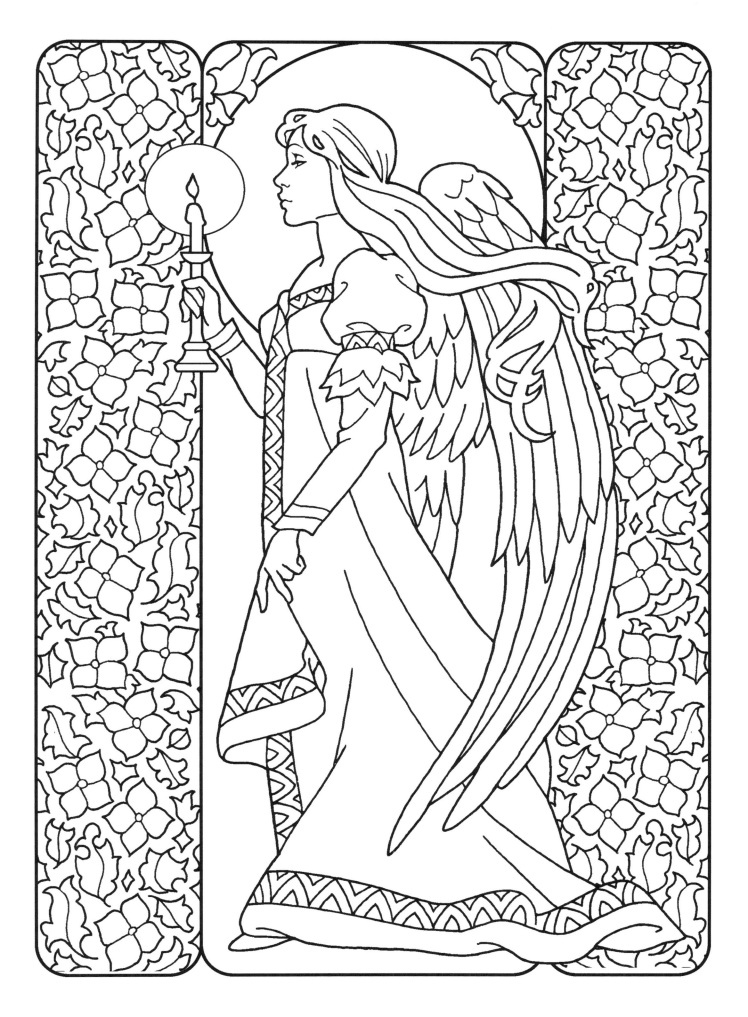

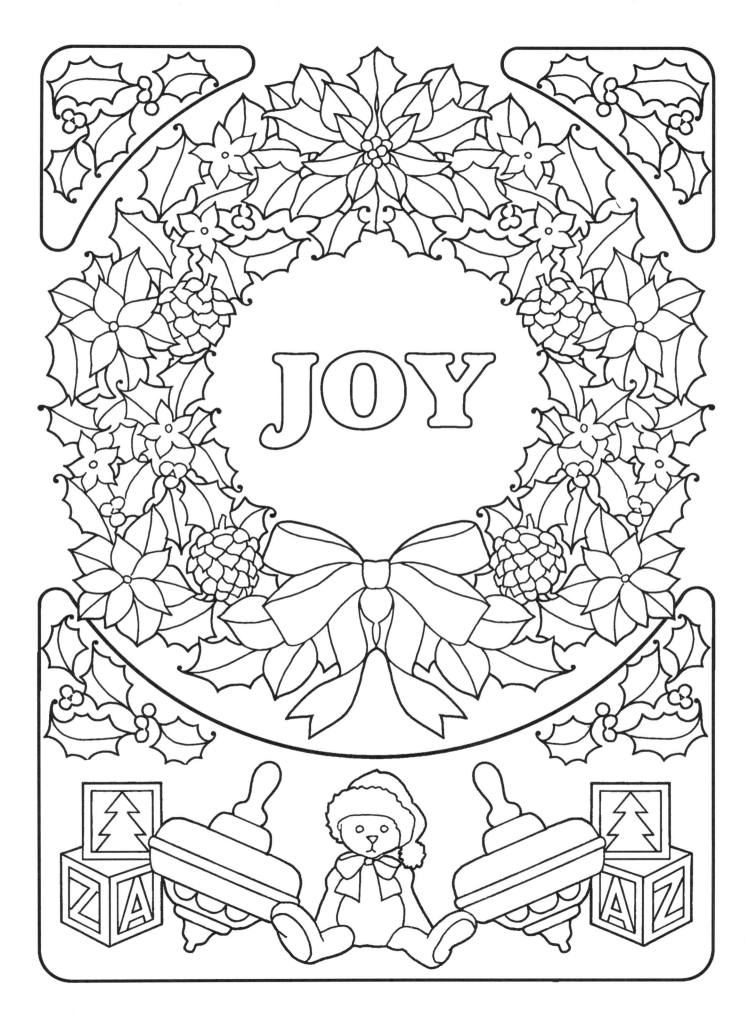

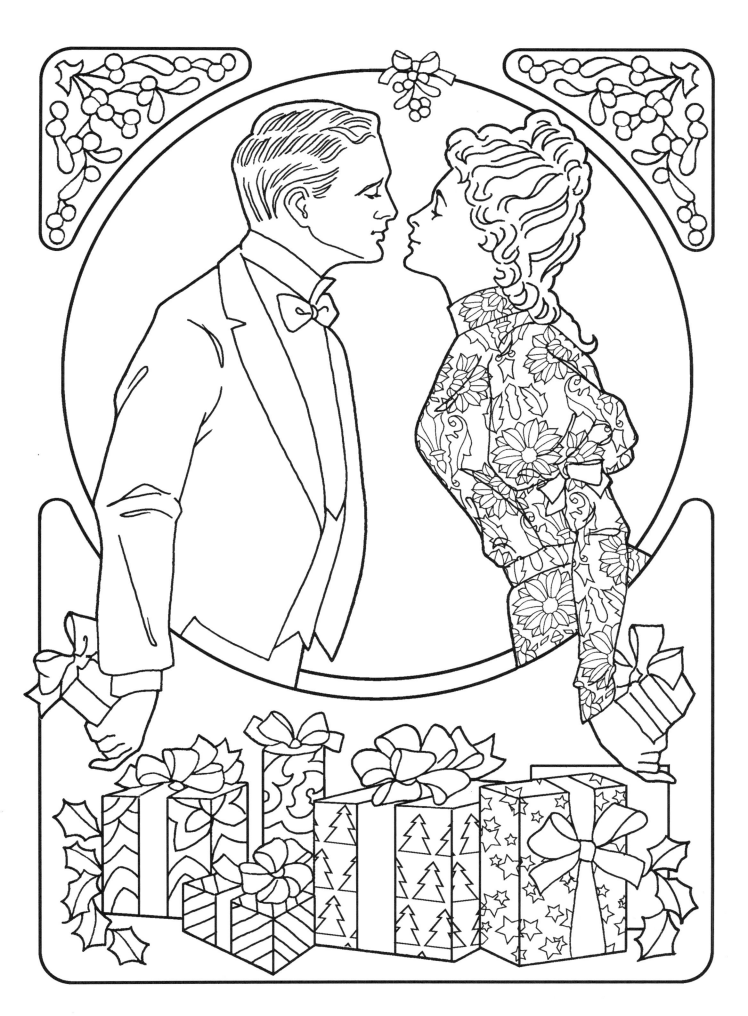

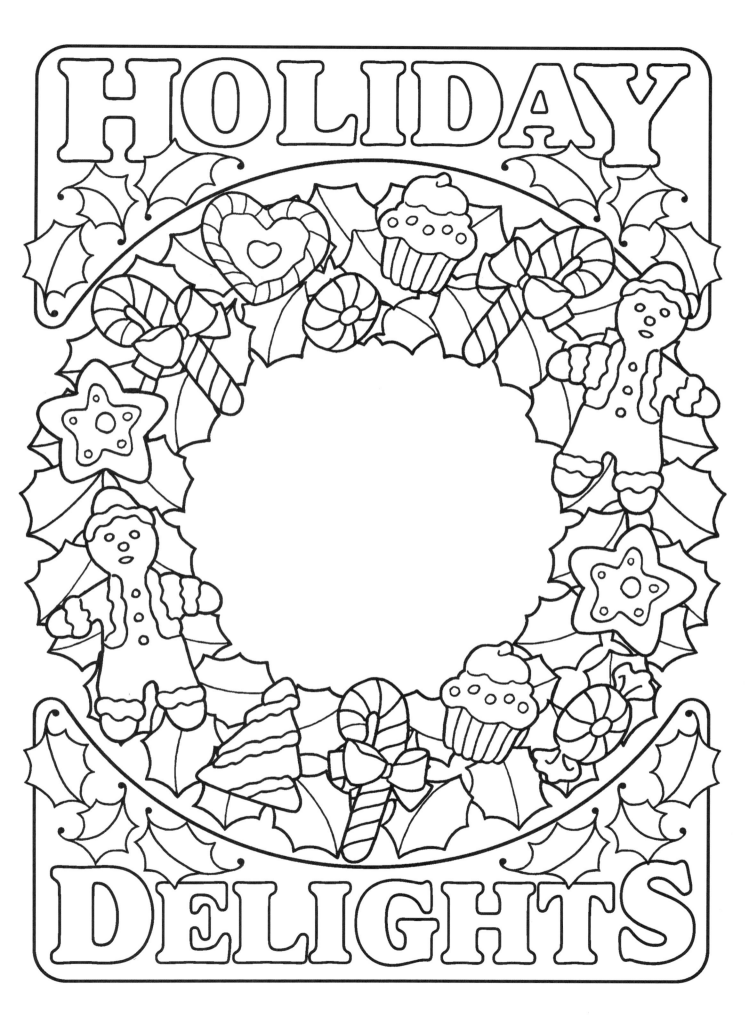

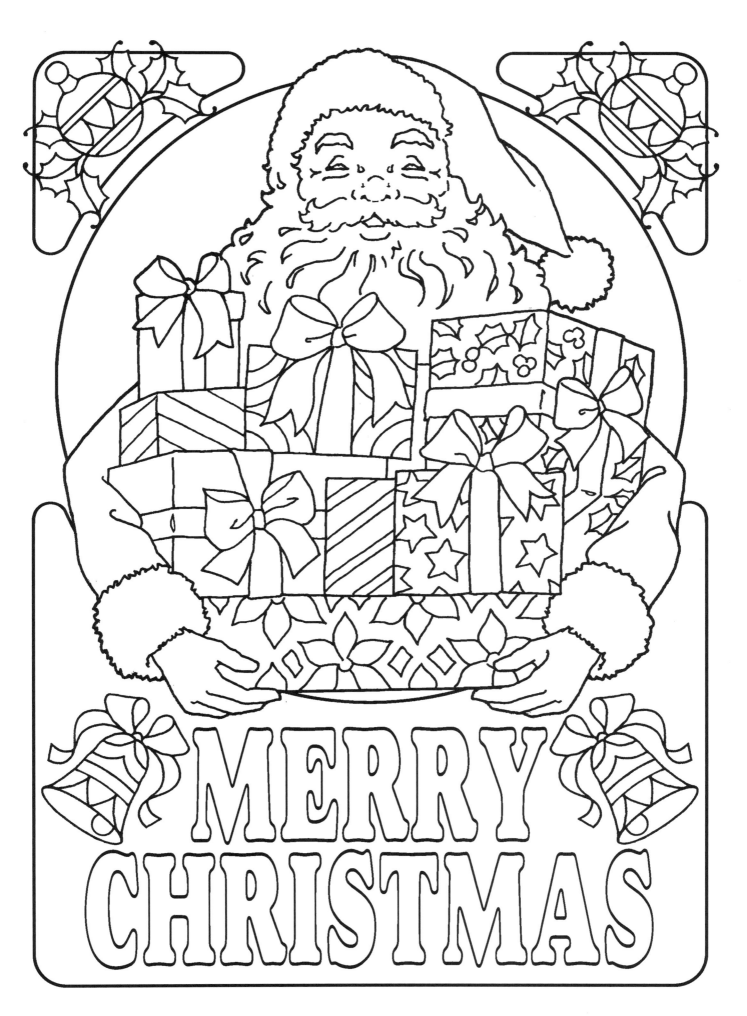

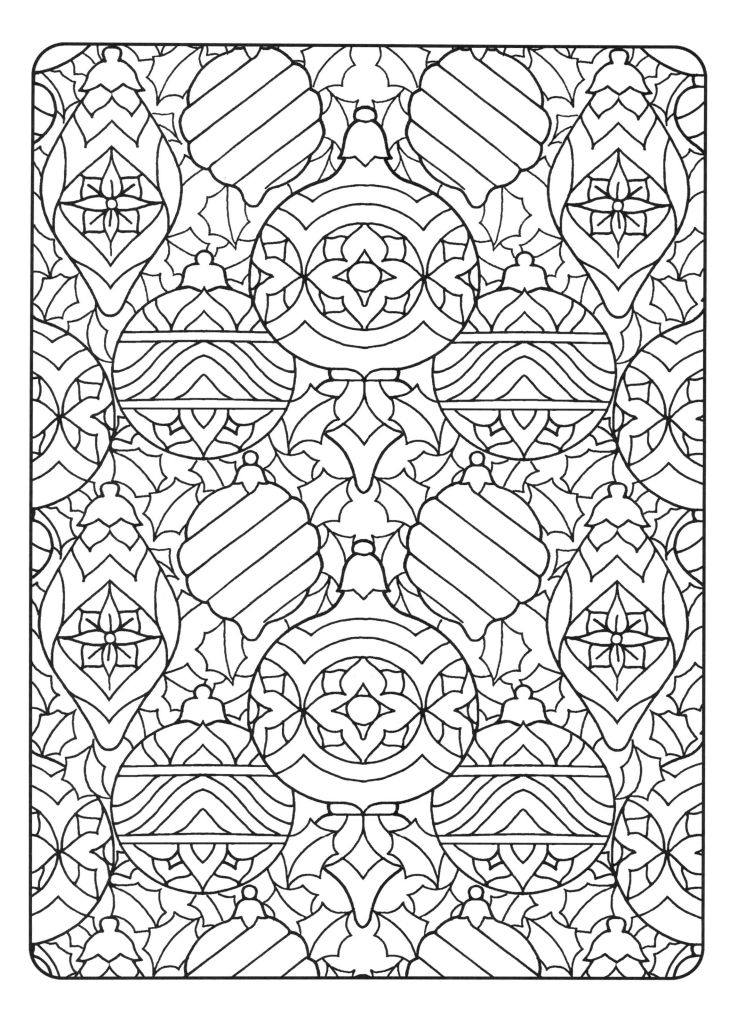

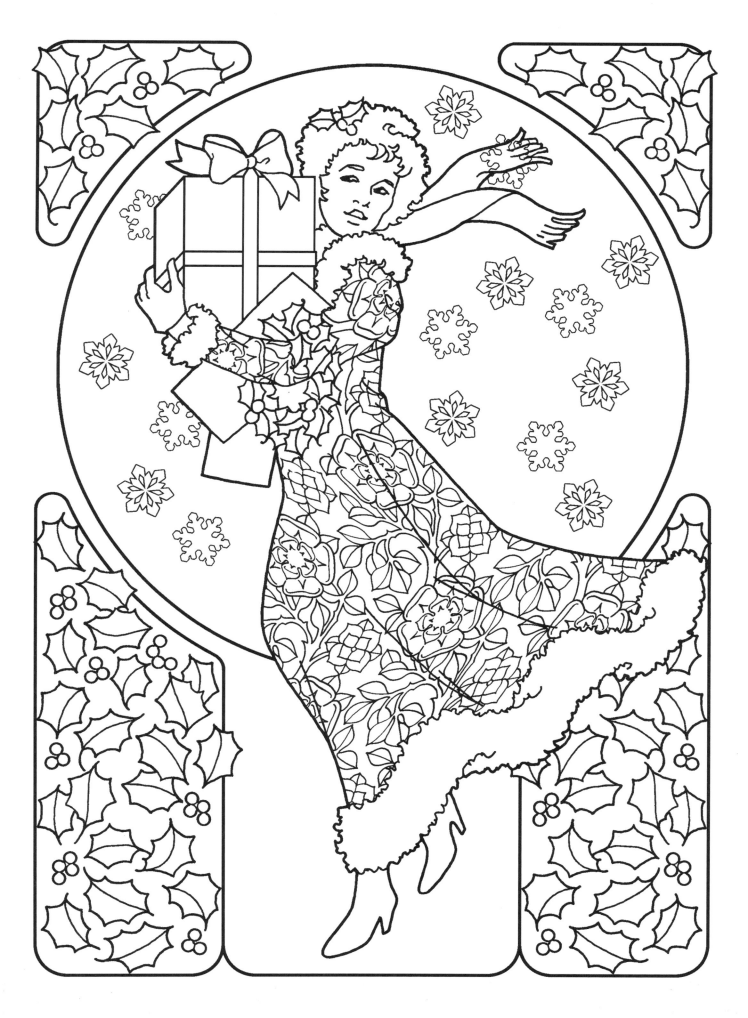

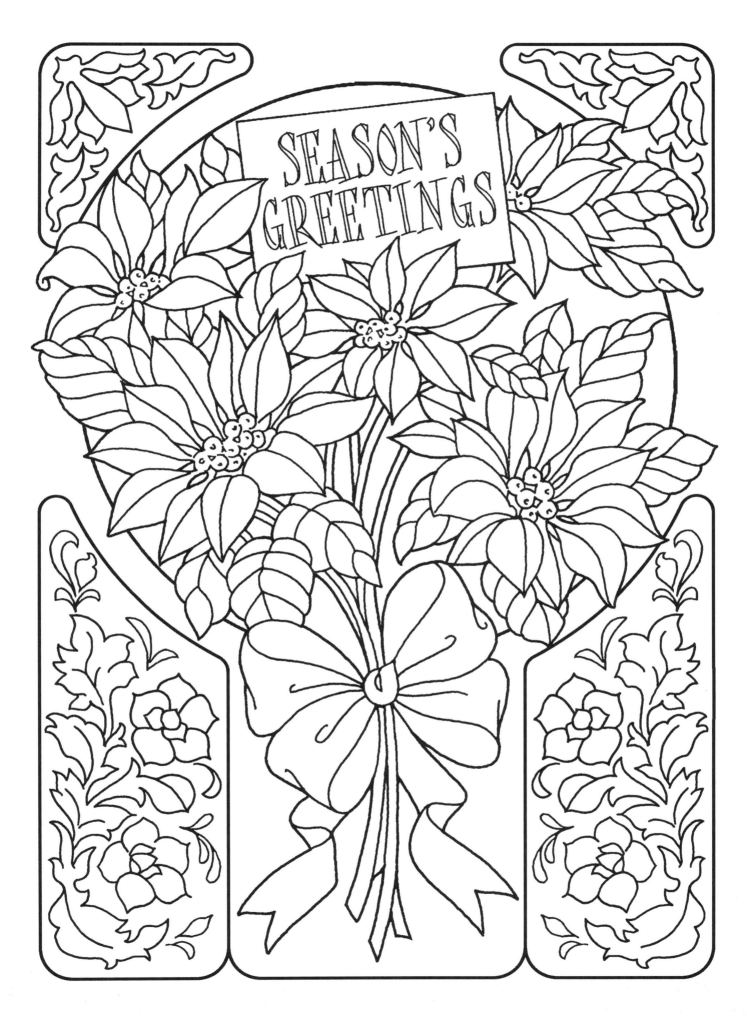

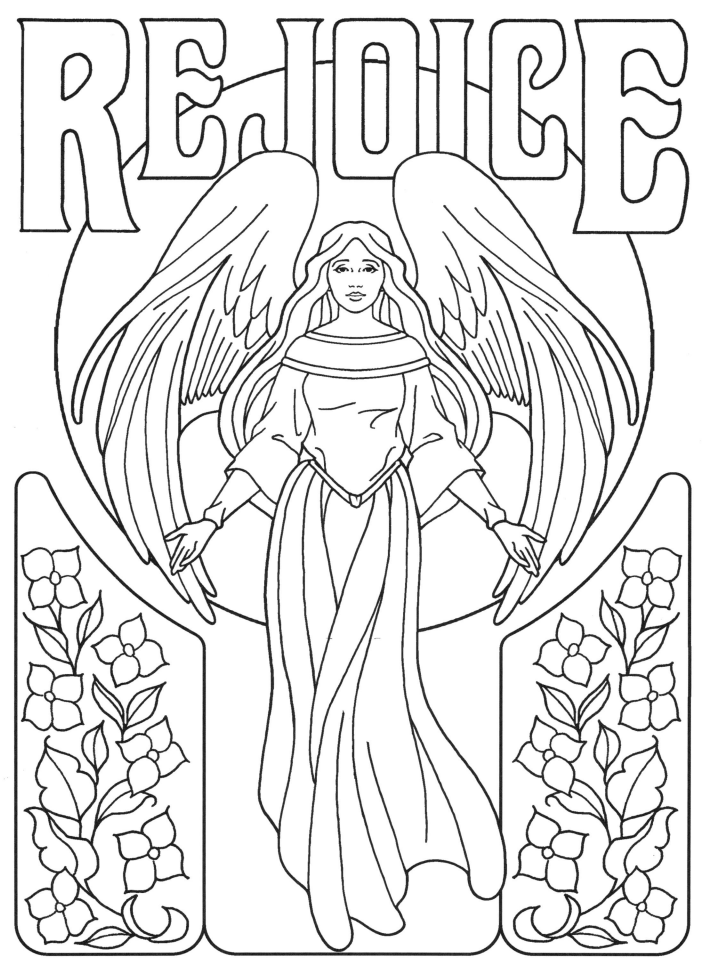

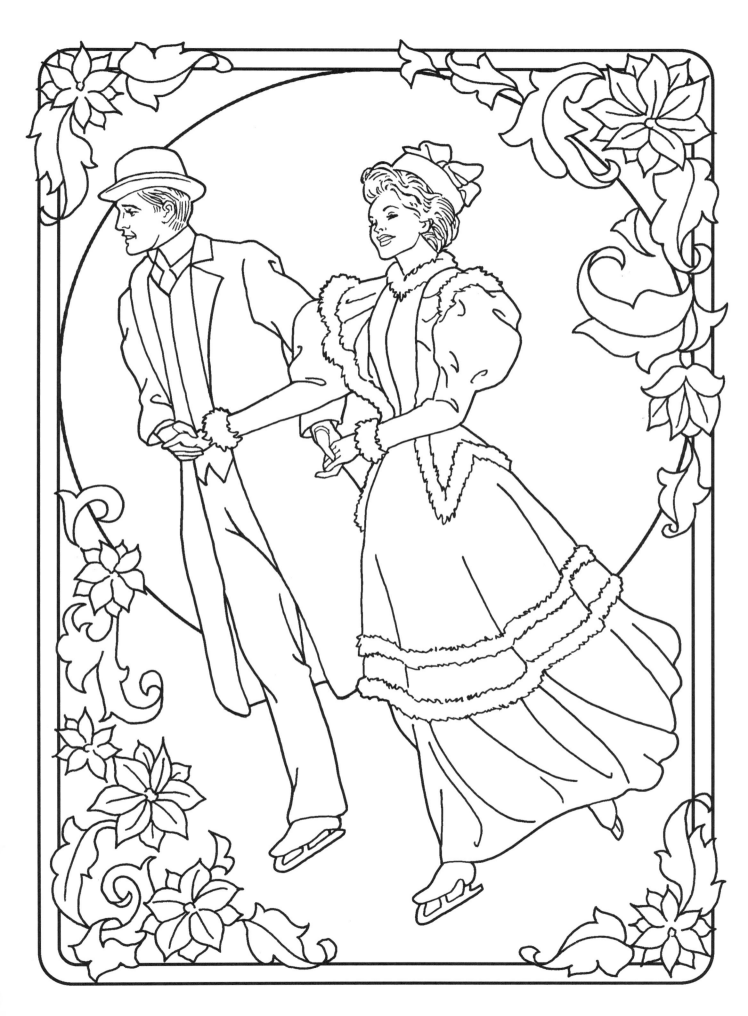

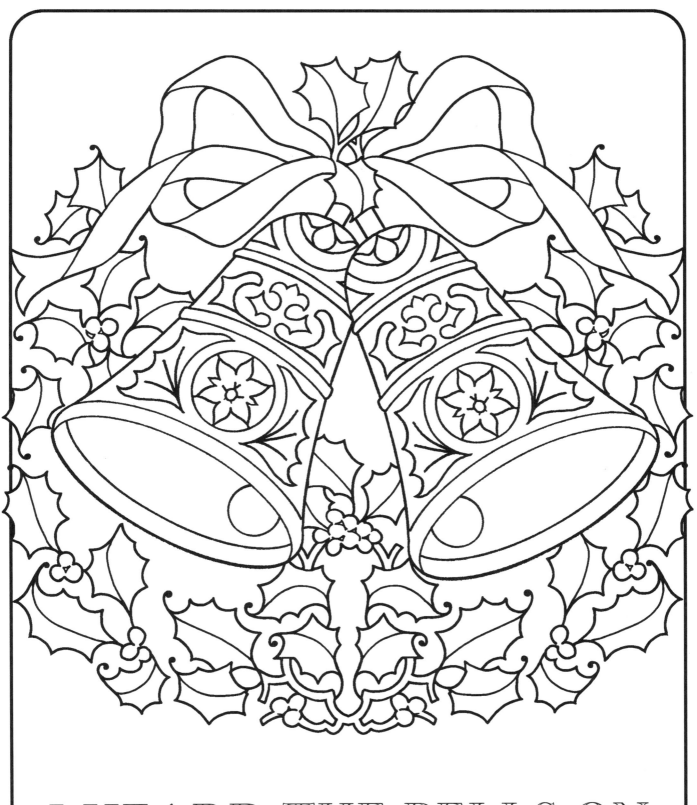

I HEARD THE BELLS ON
CHRISTMAS DAY . . .

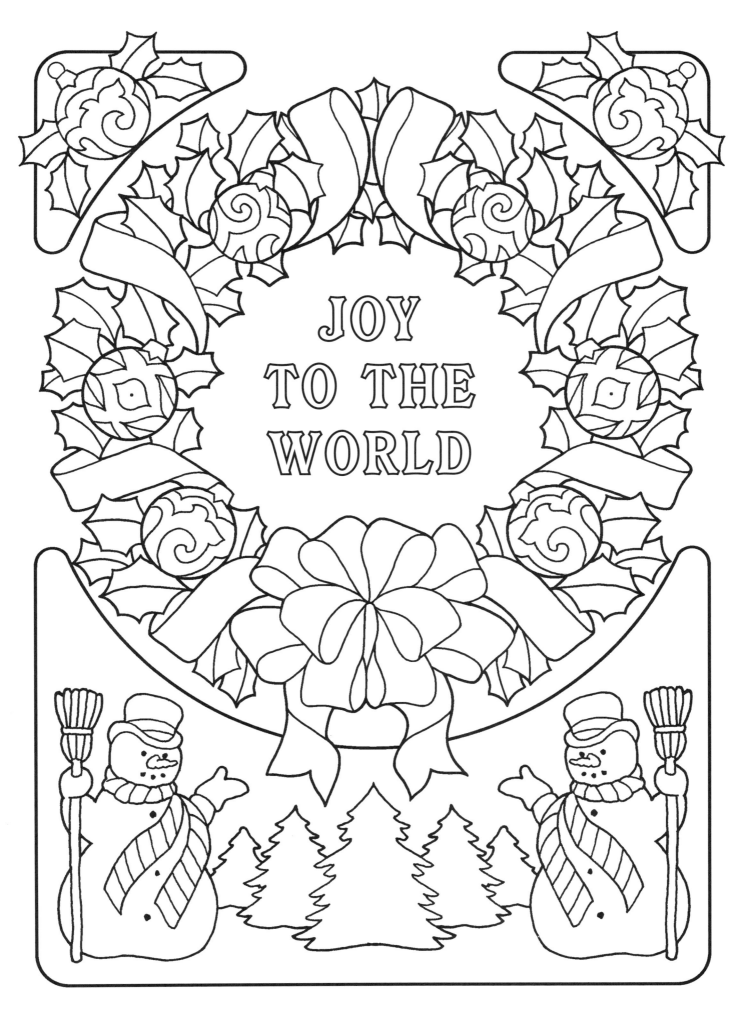

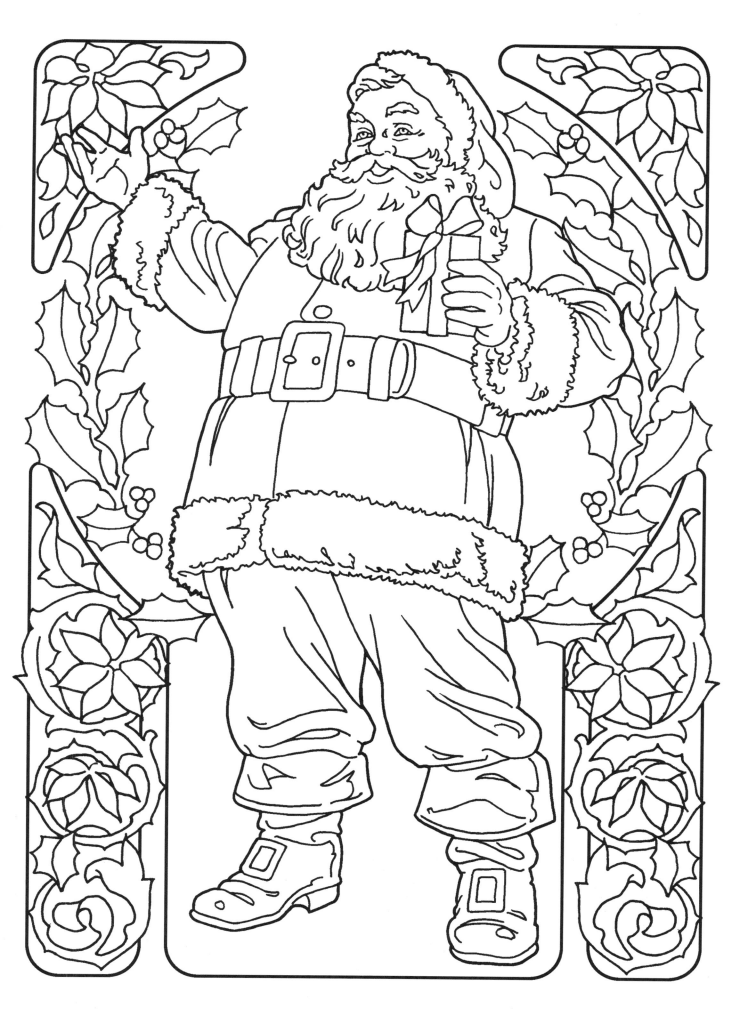

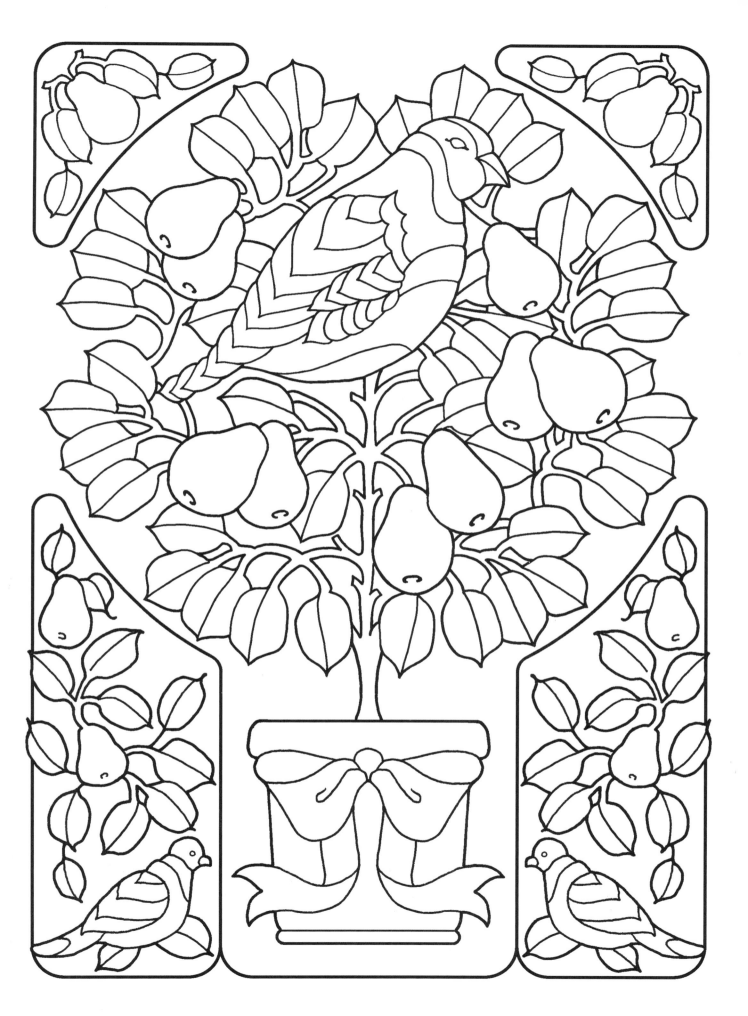

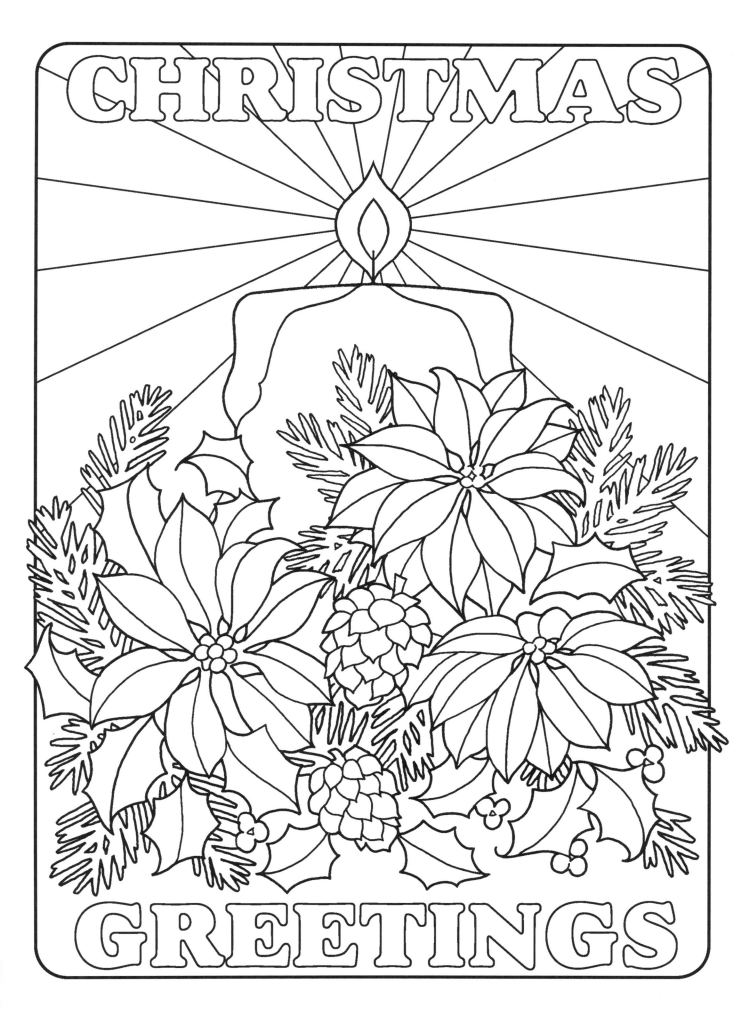

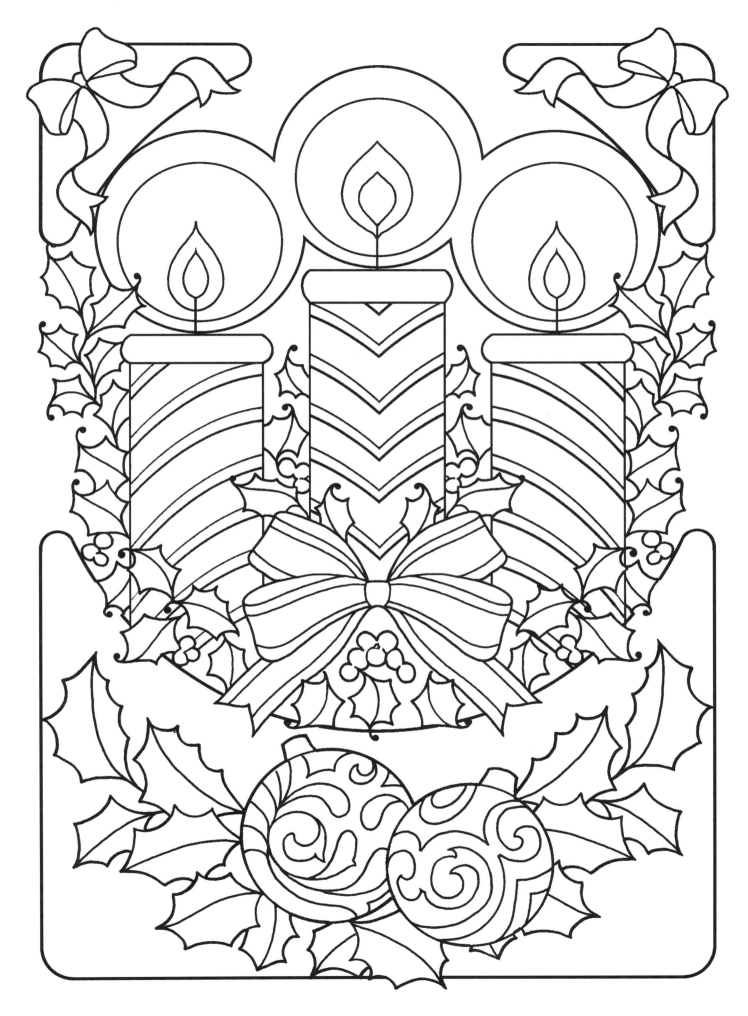

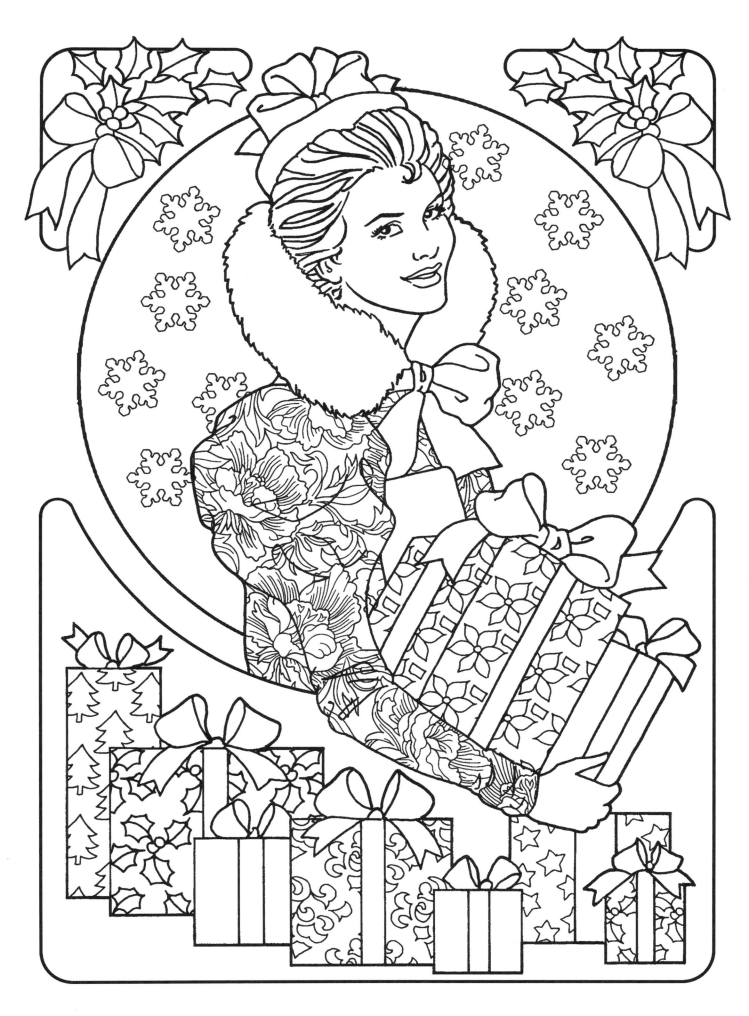

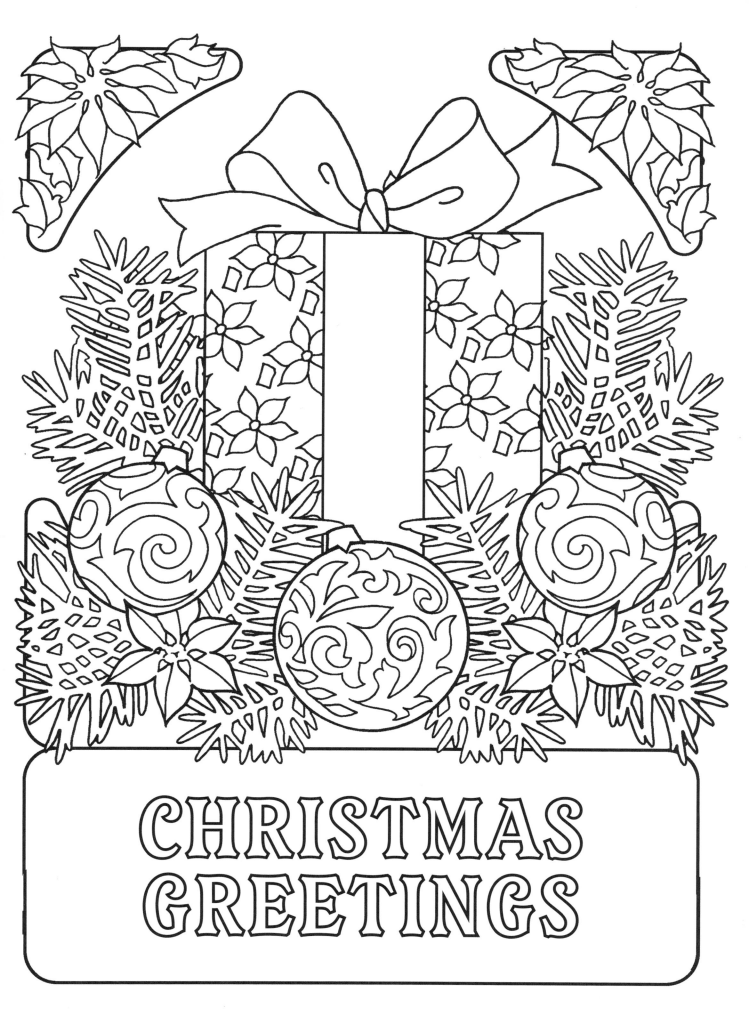

CHRISTMAS
GREETINGS

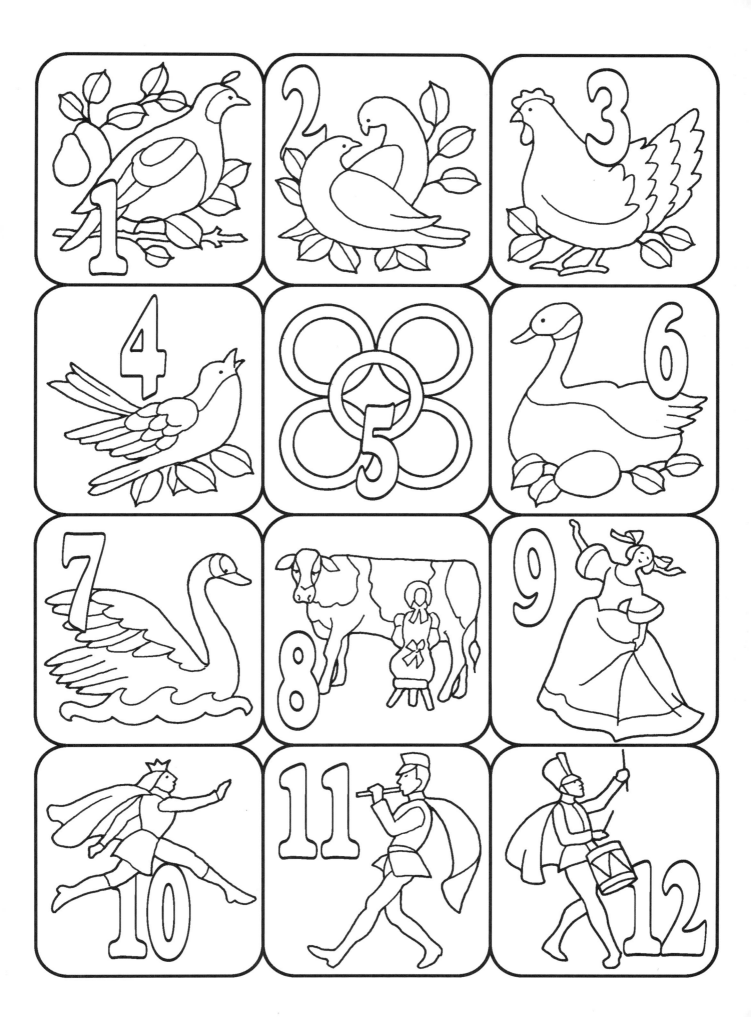

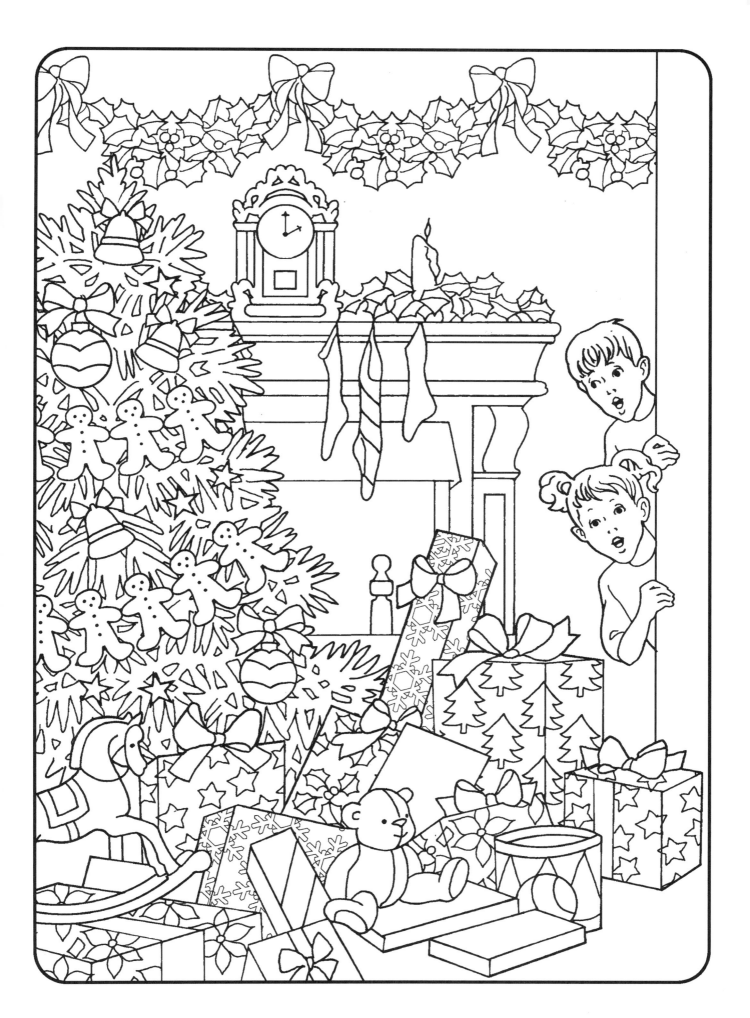

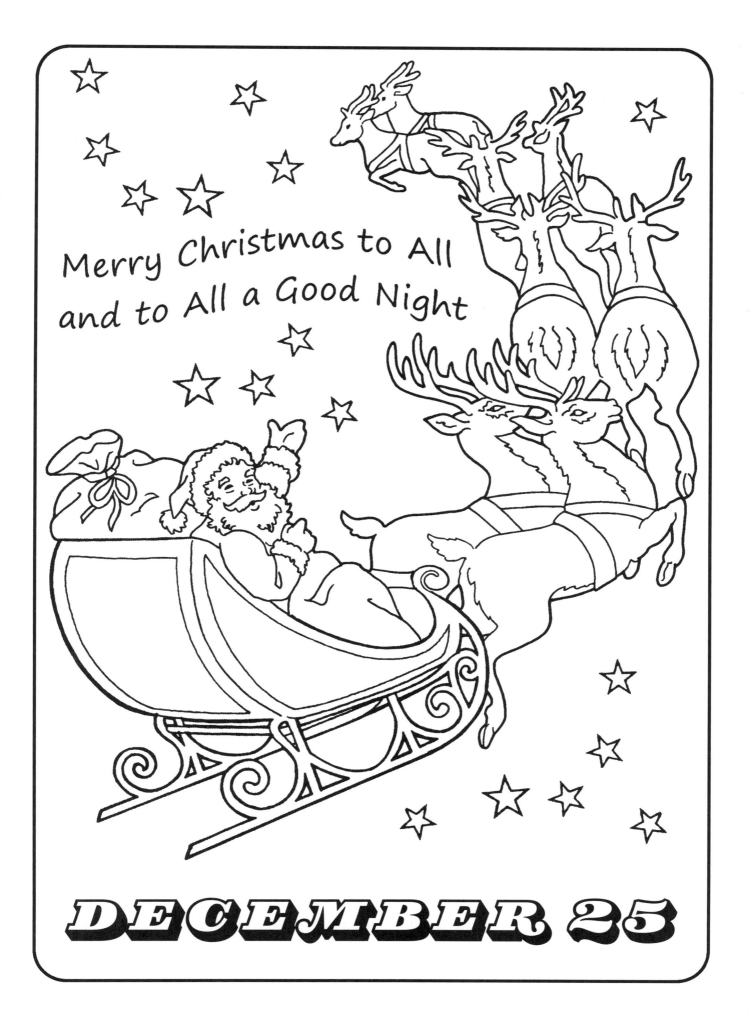

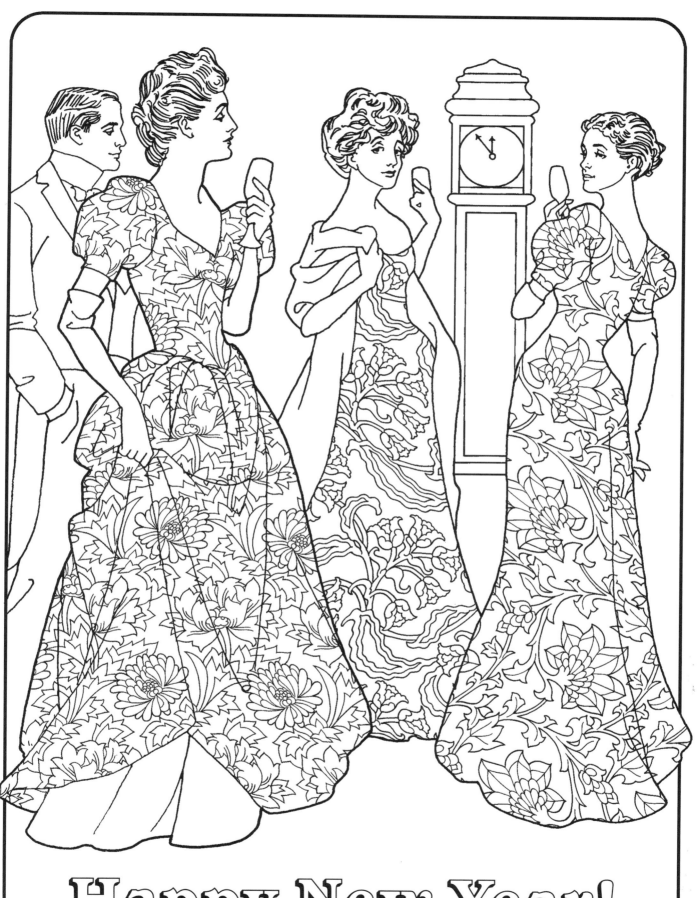

Happy New Year!